D1645612

BEST OF BRITISH!

GREAT BRITISH INVENTIONS

CLAIRE THROP

raintree

a Capstone company — publishers for children

Raintree is an imprint of Capstone Global Library Limited, a company incorporated in England and Wales having its registered office at 264 Banbury Road, Oxford, OX2 7DY – Registered company number: 6695582

www.raintree.co.uk
myorders@raintree.co.uk

Edited by Helen Cox Cannons
Designed by Ted Williams and Kazuko Collins
Original illustrations © Capstone Global Library Limited 2018
Picture research by Svetlana Zhurkin
Production by Kathy McColley
Originated by Capstone Global Library Limited
Printed and bound in India

ISBN 978 1 4747 5911 3
22 21 20 19 18
10 9 8 7 6 5 4 3 2 1

British Library Cataloguing in Publication Data
A full catalogue record for this book is available from the British Library.

Acknowledgements
We would like to thank the following for permission to reproduce photographs:
Alamy: Chronicle, 13, Paul Fearn, 26 (top), Pictorial Press Ltd, 22; Courtesy Mandy Haberman, 25; Getty Images: PA Images/Martin Keene, 15, SSPL, 20; iStockphoto: Difydave, 23, ZU_09, 9; Newscom: Heritage Images/The Print Collector, 4, 7, Mirrorpix/Crown Copyright/British Official Photograph, 19, Prisma/Album, 6, World History Archive, 12, 16, 24, Zuma Press/Kieran Galvin, 28, Zuma Press/Michael Quan, 21; Shutterstock: Andrey_Popov, 5, Crepesoles, cover (top left), Dmitriy Sandratsky, cover (top right), Georgios Kollidas, 8, J and S Photography, 14 (bottom), majeczka, 11, Monkey Business Images, 14 (top), Myotis, 27 (bottom), Passakorn sakulphan, 26 (bottom), Pavel L Photo and Video, 10, tale, cover (bottom left), travis manley, cover (bottom right), urbanbuzz, 27 (top), wisawa222, 17, Zolnierek, back cover, 18

Design Elements by Shutterstock

We would like to thank Martin Lewis for his invaluable help in the preparation of this book.

CONTENTS

Some words are shown in bold, **like this**. You can find out
what they mean by looking in the glossary.

INTRODUCTION

The island of Great Britain takes up less than half a per cent of the world's land. But British inventors have been responsible for a huge number of useful inventions, from the steam engine to concrete to **disposable** nappies.

Who gets the credit?

Many inventions are the end result of the work of lots of people over many years. This is why several different people may be listed as the inventor or creator of something, depending on where the information is found. Sometimes, the original inventor may not have had enough money to put together his or her idea. At other times, they may not have known how to! James Gregory, the first person to describe a reflecting telescope (see page 16), knew he did not have the skills to actually build it.

◀ James Gregory was a 17th-century mathematician and astronomer.

Another problem for inventors is that they might fail to take out a **patent**. A patent allows someone the sole right to sell his or her invention. If a patent does not exist, someone else could copy the idea and become known for the product, even though they did not invent it.

Sometimes no practical use can be found at the time, so an invention remains undeveloped. William Cullen, a doctor from Edinburgh, invented artificial refrigeration as far back as 1748. But it is James Harrison (another Scottish-born inventor) who is often listed as the inventor of the fridge. He came up with his version in 1851.

▼ Today, almost every home in Britain has a fridge.

INDUSTRY

During the mid-1700s and 1800s, British companies manufactured more and more, and the number of factories increased. This period in history became known as the Industrial Revolution. Some amazing inventions during this time helped work become faster and more **efficient**.

▶ Horse-drawn seed drill, 1701

Jethro Tull's seed drill helped to bring about the **agricultural revolution**. It made sowing seeds for crops much faster because it did what used to be three separate jobs in one action. It also planted three rows of seeds at one time. Farmers were then able to grow more food to sell and make more money than before. Other farmers moved to the cities to find factory work.

▼ This is an early seed drill from the 1700s. The seed drill planted evenly spaced seeds at the same depth. This meant there was less waste than when seeds were sown by hand.

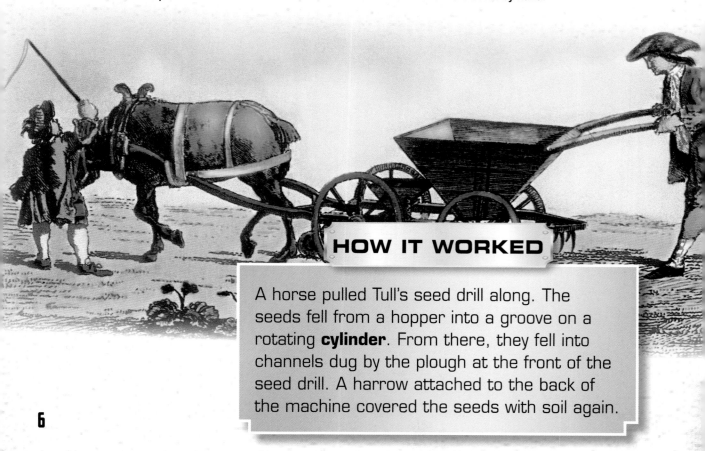

HOW IT WORKED

A horse pulled Tull's seed drill along. The seeds fell from a hopper into a groove on a rotating **cylinder**. From there, they fell into channels dug by the plough at the front of the seed drill. A harrow attached to the back of the machine covered the seeds with soil again.

JETHRO TULL (1664–1741)

Jethro Tull worked on his father's farm. There, he experimented with different farming techniques. Between 1731 and 1739, Tull wrote several books and essays to let other farmers know about his new ideas. He also invented a horse-drawn **hoe**. It could weed the crops that the seed drill had planted.

▶ Spinning jenny, 1764

James Hargreaves invented the spinning jenny. The machine made the process of cotton spinning much faster. The spinning jenny had eight **spindles,** which meant that eight threads could be spun at one time. The person operating the machine simply turned a wheel. This invention meant that people moved from spinning cotton in their own homes to working on big machines in factories.

▲ Later improvements to the spinning jenny made it possible to spin 80 threads at one time.

▶ Steam engine, 1698

In 1698, Thomas Savery developed the Miner's Friend, a basic steam engine. It helped to remove water from mines, allowing miners to dig deeper for the best coal. Steam collected in a container and shrank as it **condensed**. This left a partial **vacuum**, which caused water to be sucked up through a pipe. However, the engine wasn't able to pull water up very far, so was not much use in deeper mines.

Thomas Newcomen improved Savery's steam engine in 1712. His engine worked with a pumping action rather than a sucking action. It could pump water from much deeper mines, making it more successful than Savery's engine.

Watt's improvements

However, it was James Watt who made the real difference in 1769. His engine used 75 per cent less coal and, most importantly, it had rotating parts that allowed it to drive machinery. The steam engine quickly became Britain's main source of power. Factories no longer had to use wind or water, which were unreliable, to make their machines work.

▲ Scotsman James Watt also invented the world's first document copying machine. This was eventually replaced by modern photocopiers.

HOW IT WORKED

Steam engines use hot water to create steam. The steam causes a **piston** to move up and down inside a cylinder. Steam pushes the piston up. As it cools, the piston drops down again. As the piston moved up and down in Watt's engine, it made a lever move, which, in turn, made the machine work.

In Newcomen's engine, a spray of cold water condensed the steam. This forced the piston down into the cylinder. In Watts' engine, the piston and cylinder stayed hot because the cooling and heating process took place in a separate condensing chamber. This made it work better than Newcomen's engine.

▼ Watt's steam engine

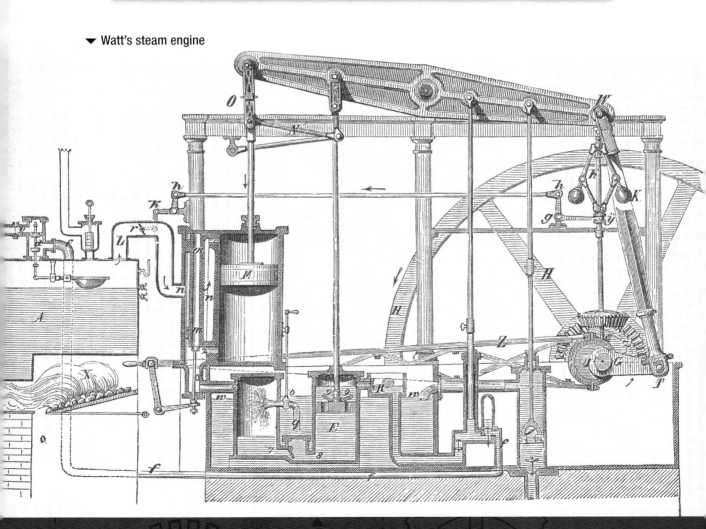

▶ Concrete, 1755–1759

In the mid-1700s, John Smeaton invented modern concrete. He added powdered brick and pebbles to **hydraulic lime cement**. This meant Smeaton's concrete was far stronger and longer lasting than the concrete the Romans used many hundreds of years before.

In 1824, another Briton, Joseph Aspdin, invented Portland cement, which is still in use today for making concrete. It was a mixture of limestone and clay burned and **ground** together. The fine powder was mixed with water, sand and gravel to make concrete. Portland cement was much easier and quicker to use because the builder didn't have to prepare the lime.

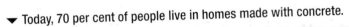

▼ Today, 70 per cent of people live in homes made with concrete.

▶ Tarmac, 1902

After buying an estate in Scotland, engineer John McAdam noticed that many of the roads were in bad shape. He experimented until he found a new way to build roads: macadamization.

Improvements

A problem with macadamization was getting the stones to stick. Surveyor Edgar Hooley found a solution. While doing his job in Derbyshire, he came across a very smooth-looking road. A barrel of tar had been spilled on it. Slag had been spread over the tar and smoothed down. Hooley spent time experimenting with mixing tar and slag and got a **patent** for tarmac (short for tarmacadam) in 1902. While Hooley's business failed, tarmac was a success: it is now used to cover roads all over the world.

▶ Anaesthetics (chloroform), 1847

Over the years, many efforts were made to reduce or remove pain for people having surgery. In 1846, the American medical student William Morton used a clear liquid known as ether to put people to sleep during surgery. But ether had some bad side effects – patients would vomit, and the liquid was highly **flammable**.

Scotsman James Young Simpson discovered the effects of chloroform after experimenting on himself and his friends at a dinner party. He realized this liquid was better and stronger than ether. Queen Victoria (1819–1901) was given chloroform while giving birth to two of her children. Her doctor, John Snow, is sometimes described as the first **anaesthetist**. He experimented on animals to find out how much chloroform to give to different people.

▼ James Young Simpson passed out after experimenting with chloroform.

▶ Antibiotics, 1928

Alexander Fleming was the scientist who made the accidental discovery of penicillin. In 1928, Fleming had been growing the **bacterium** *Staphylococcus aureus* in small dishes in his laboratory. After returning from holiday, he discovered that something had affected the bacterium. The area around the new substance was free of bacteria. After experimenting further, Fleming realized he had discovered a **mould** that could kill bacteria. He named the mould penicillin.

"Wonder drug"

In the early 1940s, the scientists Howard Florey and Ernst Chain developed penicillin so that it could be used as a drug. It is thought that at least 200 million people would have died were it not for penicillin. Women giving birth were 50 times more likely to die before penicillin was developed. Soldiers wounded in battle were also more likely to survive their injuries when treated with penicillin.

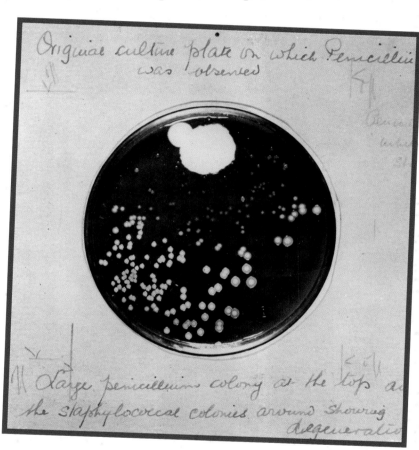

▲ This dish shows the mould that Fleming noticed on his return from holiday.

▶ Ultrasound, 1958

Professor Ian Donald from the University of Glasgow wondered if **sonar** used to locate submarines in the sea could find problems in unborn babies. Engineer Tom Brown helped Donald to create a prototype (first version) of a new machine. They used random bits and pieces, including the children's toy Meccano (see image below)! The result was the Diasonograph ultrasound machine. Ultrasound uses **sound waves** – much higher than those humans can hear – to produce pictures of the inside of the body.

HOW IT WORKS

A hand-held device called a transducer sends sound waves into the body. The sound waves hit different parts of the body, such as soft flesh or bone. These waves are reflected back to the transducer, like an echo, and on to a computer. Each part of the body sends back a different type of echo. The computer measures the distance and strength of these echoes and turns them into images, such as the picture of a baby developing in a woman's body.

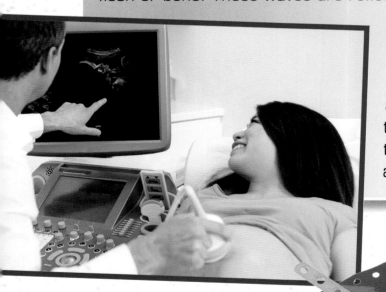

▶ Meccano

14

▶ Beta blockers (Propranolol), 1964

Scottish scientist Sir James Black created Propranolol, a type of drug called a beta blocker. Beta blockers are used to treat heart problems. They help to protect people from further heart attacks, allowing them to live longer. Beta blockers are considered one of the most important medical inventions of the 20th century. They have saved millions of lives.

◀ Sir James Black

HOW THEY WORK

Certain **hormones** in the body, such as adrenaline, can cause the heart to speed up. Beta blockers work by blocking these hormones. They slow down the activity of the heart and lower blood pressure. This allows the heart to relax.

▶ Reflecting telescope, 1668

James Gregory designed a reflecting telescope in 1663, but he was unable to actually build it. It was Sir Isaac Newton who built the first successful version. He even **ground** and polished the mirrors for it himself. Telescopes were important because they helped to prove that Earth moves around the Sun, not the other way round, as people previously believed.

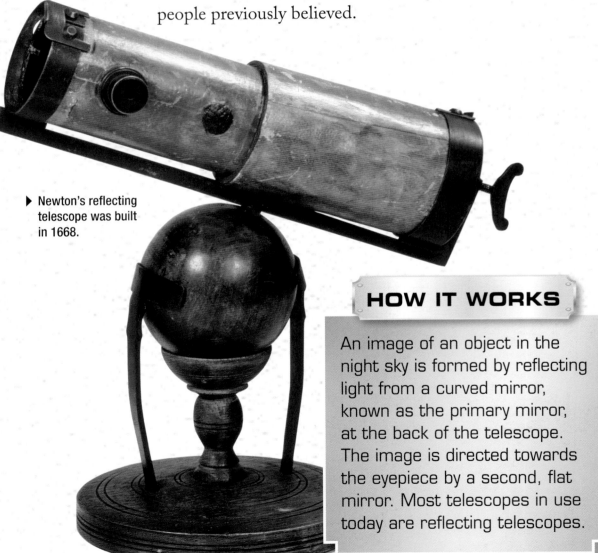

▶ Newton's reflecting telescope was built in 1668.

HOW IT WORKS

An image of an object in the night sky is formed by reflecting light from a curved mirror, known as the primary mirror, at the back of the telescope. The image is directed towards the eyepiece by a second, flat mirror. Most telescopes in use today are reflecting telescopes.

▲ Electromagnets such as this one are used in machines all over the world.

▶ **Electromagnet,** 1825

William Sturgeon revealed the world's first electromagnet in 1825. Shaped like a horseshoe, the iron bar had a copper wire wrapped around it 18 times. When an **electric current** was passed through it, it became a magnet. When the power was switched off, the iron was no longer magnetic. During his demonstration, Sturgeon showed the electromagnet (which weighed 200 grams) lifting a piece of iron weighing 4 kilograms. It was powered by a single battery.

FAST FACTS

Electromagnets allow electrical energy to control different parts in machines. This is because the magnetism can be varied in strength and switched on and off.

▲ Plastic products are now a huge part of our everyday lives.

▶ Plastic, 1862

Alexander Parkes invented Parkesine, the world's first man-made plastic. He **dissolved** a substance called nitrocellulose in alcohol and camphor (a waxy, **flammable** material). The result was a material that was easily moulded when heated but kept its shape when cold. It was the **forerunner** of celluloid, the material that films were recorded on. Parkes himself had thought Parkesine could be used in photography.

BIOGRAPHY

ALEXANDER PARKES (1813–1890)

Alexander Parkes was born in Birmingham. He worked with metals and came up with a way of **electroplating** pieces of art. Parkes had more than 66 patents for different inventions.

▶ Radar, 1935

In the years running up to World War II (1939–1945), the War Ministry approached scientist and inventor Robert Watson-Watt. The Ministry wanted Watson-Watt to investigate the "death ray" that the Germans were claiming to have invented (but actually hadn't). Watson-Watt said a death ray was impossible, but he thought he had a way to detect planes from many kilometres away using radio waves or microwaves. After a successful demonstration, he was granted a **patent**. The system wasn't actually called radar (Radio Detection And Ranging) until 1941.

HOW IT WORKS

Radar machines send out signals – **electromagnetic waves** – like those sent out by mobile phones. Radar signals are sent as short pulses. When these pulses hit an object, such as a plane, part of the radar signal reflects back to the radar machine. It is similar to when a person shouts in a cave, for example, and then hears the shout as an echo.

▼ Radar machines such as this were vital for protecting Britain from German bombers during World War II.

▶ Computer

Many people contributed to the invention of the computer, but Londoner Charles Babbage introduced the idea of a programmable "computer" in the 1820s. Sadly, money problems meant he never actually built it. The Science Museum in London later built Babbage's first computer, known as the Difference Engine, to see if it would have worked. It did! Babbage never finished his plans for the second version, the Analytical Engine.

▲ Charles Babbage's Difference Engine was a lot bigger than today's computers!

Ada Lovelace, a mathematician who worked with Babbage, is sometimes described as the world's first computer programmer. It was she who suggested that computers could have more uses than just dealing with mathematical problems.

In 1936, mathematician Alan Turing wrote about how a machine could be built to answer mathematical questions. An engineer called Tommy Flowers designed Colossus Mark 1 in 1943, with help from mathematicians at Bletchley Park in Buckinghamshire. Codebreakers were based there during World War II. Colossus was the first digital, electronic and partly programmable computer. However, it doesn't even get mentioned in early histories of computing – it was so top secret that it was destroyed after the war.

▶ World Wide Web, 1989

Tim Berners-Lee is a British scientist. He created a system that allows documents and pictures to be shared between computers all over the world. The World Wide Web has changed the way people live, allowing them to access information about anything from anywhere – well, nearly!

▲ Berners-Lee could have got a **patent** and made lots of money from his invention, but he decided to give his idea to the world for free.

▶ Lawnmower, 1830

Edwin Beard Budding got the idea for a lawnmower from cloth-cutting machines. Previously, grass was cut by hand with curved blades called scythes. Budding's lawnmower had blades that could be adjusted, just like today's mowers. It was made of wrought iron, so was very heavy. There had to be one man to push it and one to pull it. Apparently, Budding tested his lawnmower at night so that his neighbours wouldn't mock him!

▼ This illustration shows Budding with a lawnmower he invented in 1830.

▶ **Vacuum cleaner**, 1901

Hubert Booth's first **vacuum** cleaner was called Puffing Billy. It was so big it had to be moved by horse and cart and remain outside of the building being cleaned. A long hose was pushed through a window and used to suck up the dirt. Portable cleaners were available from 1906.

In 1983, Sir James Dyson invented the first bagless vacuum cleaner. After a while, vacuum cleaner bags would get clogged with dirt and dust. This would make the **suction** weak, causing the vacuum cleaner to pick up less and less dirt. Dyson came up with a solution.

HOW IT WORKS

The Dyson uses cyclonic separation. When dirty air is drawn into the vacuum cleaner, the angle it goes in causes it to spin rapidly. Larger dirt and dust particles fall to the bottom of the vacuum bin. A filter (like a sieve) then catches more dirt and dust. The air now has only the tiniest particles left in it. These spin even faster and are pushed against the sides of the bin until all the dirt falls to the bottom.

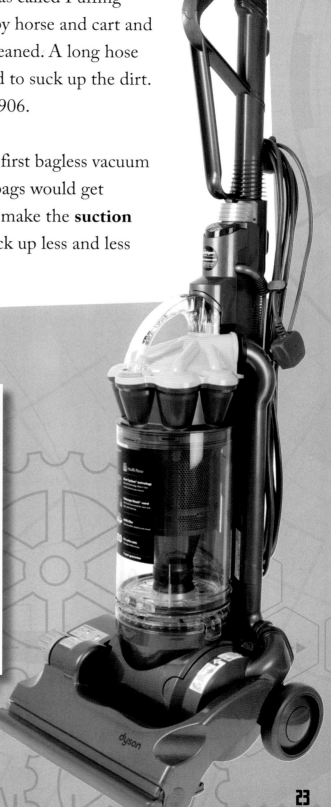

▶ The Dyson is one of the best-selling vacuum cleaners in the UK.

▶ Television, 1926

John Logie Baird built his first television with bits and bobs, including an old hatbox and a biscuit tin! In January 1926, he gave the first demonstration of a picture on a screen. Later that year, the first long-distance television signal beamed between London and Glasgow. Another first came in 1928, when Baird produced a colour television picture. He even demonstrated 3D television! At first, the BBC used Baird's mechanical system to broadcast programmes. But from the mid-1930s, his system was replaced by a better, electronic system created by another company, Marconi-EMI.

▼ Here, Baird is demonstrating one of the early versions of his televisions.

JOHN LOGIE BAIRD (1888–1946)

Baird was born in Helensburgh, Scotland. He was fascinated by the idea of inventing from a young age. When he grew up, he became a salesman, selling socks and soap. Then he decided to invent a machine that could send pictures through wires. He thought that if radio could send sound through wires, it must be possible to send pictures too. As well as the one for the television, Baird took out 178 other **patents**!

Today, nearly 5 billion people have a television. It has changed our lives, allowing us to see places we've never been, watch sport and concerts, and learn about all manner of subjects – all from the comfort of our sofa.

▶ Anywayup cup, 1996

Mandy Haberman invented the Anywayup cup, the world's first non-spill toddler training cup, after seeing a child spill blackcurrant drink over a friend's carpet. The cup has an in-built **valve** that controls the flow of liquid, stopping the flow when the child isn't drinking. When a child sucks on the cup, it lets the liquid through.

▶ Mandy Haberman and her famous Anywayup cup

EVERYDAY ITEMS

▶ Diet and exercise, 1724

In 1724, Scotsman Dr George Cheyne wrote a book called *An Essay of Health and Long Life*. In it, he suggested that a person's health would benefit from regular exercise, fresh air and avoiding luxury and foreign foods. This was the first diet book. Cheyne clearly didn't follow his own suggestions, though – he was extremely overweight! He had to travel in a specially built open-sided carriage because he couldn't fit in a normal carriage.

▲ Dr George Cheyne

▶ Matches, 1826

John Walker was a chemist from Stockton-on-Tees. While experimenting, he dipped the end of a stick into some chemicals. When he scraped it across the hearth at home, it produced a flame. He had invented the first match. Walker's "Friction Lights" went on sale in 1827 and were sold with a piece of sandpaper for striking.

▲ Modern matches

▶ Chocolate, 1847

J. S. Fry & Sons Ltd. was a chocolate company founded in 1761. Originally, people drank hot chocolate. In 1847, Fry's company created the world's first solid chocolate bar by adding extra cocoa butter. In 1866, Fry's produced the first brand of chocolate bar (Fry's Chocolate Cream).

▼ Fry's Chocolate Cream bars are still being sold today.

▶ Disposable nappy, 1947

After Valerie Hunter Gordon had her third child, she decided she was fed up with washing nappies. She tried to buy **disposable** ones, but couldn't find them in the shops. So she invented them herself! The first ones were made of old parachutes, tissue padding and cotton wool. In 1948, she took out a **patent** for "Paddis". They were very popular until an American company, Pampers, began to sell disposable nappies in Britain during the 1960s.

◀ Today, disposable nappies like this one are very common.

CONCLUSION

There are many inventions by British men and women that are now part of our everyday lives. And there are 25,000 **patents** taken out every year in Britain. In 2004, Natalie Ellis invented the Road Refresher dog bowl, which allows dogs to drink without spilling water everywhere, even when travelling in a vehicle. Michael Pritchard developed the portable Lifesaver water filter in 2006. It allows people to clean any water they find so that it is drinkable.

Not just for adults!

It's not just adults having all the inventing fun. Sam Houghton was only three when he came up with the idea of a double-headed broom. He had been watching his dad swap brooms to sweep up leaves and then dirt. He was inspired to tie the two brooms together, back to back. He is the youngest person in Britain to take out a patent.

▼ Inventions can be useful or they can be fun! The British have invented many of the world's top sports, including football.

TIMELINE

1668 Reflecting telescope

1698 Steam engine (Savery)

1701 Horse-drawn seed drill — **1700**

1712 Steam engine (Newcomen)

1724 Diet and exercise —

1748 Artificial refrigeration

1755–1759 Concrete

1764 Spinning jenny —

1769 Steam engine (Watt)

1800

1810s–1820s Macadamization

1820s Difference Engine (computer)

1824 Portland cement —

1825 Electromagnet

1826 Matches —

1830 Lawnmower

1847 Chocolate —

1847 Anaesthetics (chloroform)

1862 Parkesine, world's first man-made plastic

1901 Vacuum cleaner — **1900** — 1902 Tarmac

1926 Television —

1928 Antibiotics

1935 Radar —

1943 Colossus Mark 1 (computer)

1947 Disposable nappy —

1958 Ultrasound

1964 Beta blockers (Propranolol) —

1983 Bagless vacuum cleaner

1989 World Wide Web —

1996 Anywayup cup

2004 Road Refresher dog bowl — **2000**

2006 Lifesaver water filter

29

GLOSSARY

agricultural revolution in the 1700s, a change in the way farming was carried out, from a traditional method to more modern, machine-led farming

anaesthetist person who gives patients anaesthetics before surgery

bacterium tiny living thing; a group of them is called bacteria. Some are useful but others can cause disease.

condense change from gas to liquid

cylinder tube-shaped object

disposable item that is used once and then thrown away

dissolve when a solid or a gas mixes with a liquid so well that it disappears

electric current flow of electricity through a wire

electromagnetic wave wave of energy that travels at the speed of light and has magnetic and electric properties

electroplating covering an object in a thin layer of metal, such as silver, by passing an electric current through the object

flammable can easily catch fire

forerunner something that does something first before another thing

ground shaped or reduced the thickness of a material

hoe gardening tool used for weeding

hormone naturally occurring chemical in your body, which makes an organ in the body do something

hydraulic lime cement type of cement that can set under water; the more hydraulic a lime is, the faster it sets and the better its strength

mould type of fungus that grows in damp or warm conditions

patent legal document that gives one person or company the right to produce a particular invention

piston small tube that moves up and down inside a larger tube to generate power

sonar equipment that uses sound waves to work out the depth of the sea or where an underwater object is

sound wave wave or vibration that can be heard

spindle rod in a machine around which another part of the machine turns

suction process in which substances are sucked out of something

vacuum completely empty space

valve device that controls the flow of a liquid

Books

50 Things You Should Know About: Inventions, Clive Gifford (QED, 2016)

100 Inventions That Made History (Dorling Kindersley, 2014)

Greatest Inventions of All Time, Jillian Powell (Wayland, 2016)

Websites

www.bbc.co.uk/education/clips/zx9c87h
Find out what it takes to be a good inventor!

www.dkfindout.com/uk/science/amazing-inventions/telescope
Find out more about the reflecting telescope and Sir Isaac Newton.

PLACES TO VISIT

Museum of Science and Industry
Liverpool Road
Manchester M3 4FP
www.msimanchester.org.uk
Visit this museum to see steam engines in action.

The National Museum of Computing
Block H
Bletchley Park
Milton Keynes MK3 6EB
www.tnmoc.org
Learn about the history of computing and see a rebuilt version of Colossus.

National Museum of Scotland
Chambers Street
Edinburgh EH1 1JF
www.nms.ac.uk/national-museum-of-scotland
Find out more about the history of Scotland's inventors in this museum. There is also a Watt steam engine on show.

INDEX